RECENT RHYMING RAMBLES

Mirador Publishing
Mirador
Wearne Lane
Langport
Somerset
TA10 9HB

Recent Rhyming Rambles

By

Jan Millward

Also by the author

Tiny Caring Gestures
Gentle Sweet Reminders
Ssh... It Happens! Rural Rhymes from Ryme Intrinseca
Shh... It Happened Again! More Rural Rhymes

Introduction

This is my fifth book of poetry and it is a real mixture of my life experiences. There are a sprinkling of rural poems and a smattering about care.

I have blended in some of life's petty irritations and balanced it with some of the events that have moulded and shaped my life.

It is sometimes more bramble than ramble, but hopefully I will have made you laugh and reflect on this peculiar shared journey that we call life!

Love.

Love is in the things unsaid,
the early morning tea in bed.
A gentle touch when you are stressed,
the healing hugs that are the best.

The meal prepared when you get home,
the knowing that you're not alone.
The sifting of words said in haste,
the challenges together faced.

The umbrella in the rain,
the love heart hanging on a chain.
The worried look when you feel ill,
the jacket to ward off the chill.

Love shows itself in many ways,
the tiny spark becomes a blaze.
The little gestures go unspoken,
healing hearts that once were broken.

And if you find love, hold on tight.
Cherish it with all your might.
Respect each other's point of view,
and always be forever true.

Love is a treasure rare and pure,
it can't be bought, it has no cure.
It is the greatest gift on earth,
if you can recognise its worth.

The Post Christmas Diet.

We all do it. Every year we overindulge on lots of lovely treats over Christmas and immediately regret it on January 1st!

Christmas is now over and my clothes are feeling tight,
and a glance caught in a mirror has given me a fright.
I've eaten all the toffees, the shortbread and mince pies,
the cheeses with the crackers have migrated to my thighs.

The turkey and the stuffing, the home cooked ham and crisps.
I've mulled on wine and sherry as they gurgled past my lips.
I've picked at mounds of chocolates 'til I cannot see my feet,
and chosen all the toffees from tins of Quality Street.

The Christmas pud' with brandy and a great big slice of stollen,
it's really not surprising that my stomach's fat and swollen.
The cocktails, tasty nibbles and trifles topped with cream,
I have eaten far too many, now I'm bursting every seam.

I might go on a diet, and become a member of a gym.
But I must eat all the goodies up before I try to slim.
I'm told I must make smoothies out of broccoli and leeks,
but looking at my figure, I'll be doing it for weeks.

It really is bad weather, or I could go for a run,
I would try counting calories, but it's really not much fun.
I've had a go at Zumba and I bought a half price rower,
but if I was a three toed sloth, I couldn't go much slower.

If it snows I'll take up skiing or I'll buy myself a bike.
I'll have nothing but a milk shake, morning, noon and night.
It really is depressing, this needing to lose weight,
so I'll try to not look desperate with one carrot on my plate.

I'll try and eat the healthy stuff, the cabbage and the kale.
If you offer me a chocolate, then I'll try not to inhale.
I'll fight my losing battle with elastic round my waist.
It's really such a conflict that I suffer from good taste!

Caller 45.

It is so frustrating to be stuck in a queue on the telephone and not being able to talk to a real person!

Thank you for calling our helpline,
you are 45th in the queue.
All our phone lines are busy
and there's nothing else you can do.

Please hold the line and be patient,
we'll answer as soon as we're free.
We suggest you make yourself comfy,
and have a nice cup of tea.

We're sorry that you're still holding,
we've chosen some music for you.
Please don't swear at your mobile,
we're recording everything blue.

It's a shame you don't like canned Mozart,
we thought it quite classy and bright.
We used to play three hours of Reggae,
but we don't want to get in a fight.

Congratulations for listening,
you've moved up two places at last.
It won't be for very much longer,
so chin up and don't feel downcast.

Our operators are all very busy,
they're having some coffee and cake.
We thank you for being so patient,
it will only be a short break.

Thank you so much for calling,
we value your custom and wit.
We listened in on you shouting,
please don't call our boss an old git.
Bravo! You are now moving,
you only have two hours to wait.
There's no point shouting and screaming,
you'll get yourself into a state.

Thank you again valued client,
it's getting quite late in the day.
We'll be closing up in ten minutes,
maybe you could try to pray?

We're sorry to have to inform you,
we are all now on our way home.
It's pointless you sitting there trying,
we've switched off the lights and the phone.

Please try again in the morning,
don't throw the phone in disgust.
Your blood pressure will keep on rising,
and you can't ring if you go bust!

The Old Fart.

I can't write a book of poetry without mentioning my dear husband. This poem however, is possibly not what he was hoping I would mention!

I love my darling husband,
this is written from the heart.
But he can be so disgusting,
when he is trying to fart.

He never will admit it,
he will blame the nearest dog.
Even though the air is heavy,
with his smelly stinking fog.

He pops them out in cafés
and looks round in mock disgust.
If someone lights a matchstick,
I fear we may combust.

The worst are silent and deadly.
They stink beyond belief.
He sits there smiling sweetly,
with a faint look of relief.

And when we are both sleeping,
I'm awoken with a start.
It sounds just like a shotgun,
the unguarded bed time fart.

And I know that I'm in trouble
if he's been eating curry,
I leave the windows open
so I don't have to worry.

And if we are out driving
along the open road,
he'll blame the local farmers
for spilling part of their load.

I've learned to spot the signals,
the casual sideways look.
The little shift whilst sitting,
eyes raised above his book.

He never will admit it
and I often get the blame,
I just hope he's never sitting
by an unguarded open flame.

The Dentist.

I don't know of anyone who enjoys a visit to the dentist and the visits seem to be getting more frequent and expensive as I get older!

I've an appointment with the dentist,
I have to have a filling.
I hate to have to listen
to the high-pitched whine of drilling.

I wait with trepidation,
and read a magazine.
It's about the coronation,
full of pictures of the Queen.

I have a glance around me,
there's a young girl on the phone.
She's been waiting ages and
she's rung her Dad to have a moan.

I can smell the disinfectant,
or it might be blue mouthwash.
And I glance at a big poster
showing the right way to brush.

I am getting a little bit nervous
and I feel the need to cough,
though my teeth are fresh and minty
and I've flossed the small bits off.

A nurse walks down the hallway,
she's calling out my name.
My tooth has now stopped hurting
and I'm wondering why I came.

The dentist has a mask on
and he asks me how I am,
just as my tongue discovers
that wayward bit of ham.

I sit on the shiny recliner,
I'm at the point of no return.
I smile at him quite sweetly,
but he's looking rather stern.

And then he tilts me backwards,
like a Thunderbird on go,
sliding swiftly downhill,
until I have to shout out Whoa!

He says that he is going
to drill a hole into my tooth.
I should have been more careful
when I was still a youth.

He says he'll dig the bad out,
put amalgam in the hole.
Then I'll rinse out with blue water
and spit out in the bowl.

He fills a big syringe up
and injects my poor old gum.
It feels like my mouth is swelling
and my tongue is going numb.

I look up to the ceiling
and read posters about brushing.
How to floss the bits out,
there is no gain in rushing.

The nurse gives me some goggles
and a bib to catch the blood,
she uses a noisy sucker
to catch the rising flood.

The dentist starts the drilling,
he says he'll stop if I feel pain.
I can't grit my teeth and bear it,
so I fear it's all in vain.

I feel the water building
and choking is a worry.
My nose has started itching,
(I just wish that he would hurry).

I keep stretching my mouth open
as I look right up his nose.
I try to avoid eye contact,
but swallow the suction hose.

And then it is all over
and the words I want to hear:
"Don't come back until next August,"
(I give an inward cheer).

I promise to keep on brushing
and attacking all that plaque,
especially if it means that he's happy
and he doesn't want me back.

I walk back to the car park.
I'm feeling quite sedated.
I suck a bar of chocolate
then I'm feeling quite elated.

And yes, I'll have to go back.
I know he will tut and say:
"We need to have some x rays,
it will be a bit more to pay."

So I take out a small mortgage
to cover all the costs,
but I'm grateful that it's all over
and I've kept more teeth than I've lost!

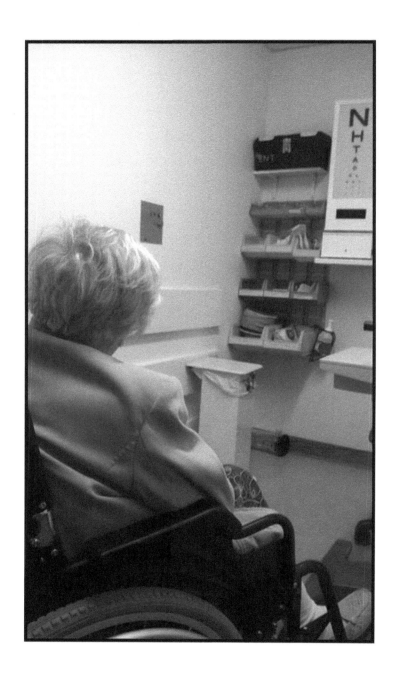

A and E.

This poem is based on a recent experience when I had to take my elderly mother in to A and E after a fall. We were there for hours.

There's nothing that is worse for me
than a little trek to A and E.
I've been there for too many trips
with my old dad and his dodgy hips.

I went there when my mum fell over
and when my son got bitten by Rover.
We've had our share of odd mishaps;
we've tripped on steps and fell through gaps.

I had to go when I banged my head;
I would have rather stayed in bed.
But sometimes life can be unkind
and you just have to be resigned.

The badly hurt are treated first,
the rest of us just feel we're cursed.
A sign goes round the waiting room,
a four hour wait fills us with gloom.

They check us in, and then we must wait
for them to tell us what's our fate.
The room fills up with fractured bones
and teenage kids using their phones.

We sit and hope that we'll be next
and send our friends a gory text.
A worried mother and her child
gets rushed on through, we sit beguiled.

A man demands he must be seen,
they take him through behind a screen.
The vending machine with tempting drinks,
eats up our coins, it's on the blink.

A cleaner looking rather grim,
shuffles through and checks the bin.
Then finally we see a nurse,
she says we're lucky, she's seen it worse.

Last night they queued right out the door
and some were sitting on the floor.
She asks our name and why we're here,
then spots the bandage round the ear.

And back we go to wait our turn,
we've past the point of no return.
Then just when we dash for the loo,
they call our name and walk us through.

A doctor with a stethoscope,
washes his hands with liquid soap.
He checks to see what he can do
and wants to get a better view.

So next a wait for X rays follow;
it won't be long 'till it's tomorrow.
And back we go and wait some more,
staring at the same old floor.

And then the news we came to hear,
the X rays say that all is clear.
We can go home, we will survive.
It sure feels good to be alive.

Next time you go to A and E
with a bad throat or dodgy knee,
remember patience is required
and you might go home very tired.

But they are there to help us out,
so please don't scream at them or shout.
Thanks to the doctors and the nurses
who put up with the daily curses.

We're grateful for our NHS,
they sort us out when we're a mess.
We'll try to stay away next time,
but thanks to them we now feel fine!

Superstitions.

We are a funny lot. We may think we don't care about superstitions, but most of us will recognise at least some of these!

Don't walk under a ladder or you are tempting fate.
Nod or salute to that magpie that's sat on your garden gate.
Don't put new shoes on a table, and remember to touch wood.
Throw spilt salt o'er your shoulder, if you want your life to be good.

And if your foot is itching it means you're going away,
(unless it is the left one and then you'll have to stay).
Make a wish with a wishbone and hope they all come true.
But never cross on a staircase, it's something you must not do.

If you find a horseshoe, you must hang it the right way up.
If it is pointing downwards you're sure to run out of luck.
Pick some lucky white heather and keep it in a jar,
then hope a black cat walks towards you, if you want to go far.

Be careful with your mirrors or for seven years you will cry,
and never catch a sparrow if you really don't want to die.
And when you're getting married you must wear something blue,
as well as something borrowed and something that's brand new.

You must never open a brolly until you have got outside.
Because you won't get through the doorway, so that is justified.
If you hear someone sneezing it's best to say "bless you,"
and make sure you cross your fingers so all your dreams come
true.

On the first of the month say "white rabbits," then give a pinch and
a punch.
And don't step on the cracks in the pavement when you're out for
lunch.
And if you get hit with bird poo, it's said you'll get good luck,
although all that has really happened is that you are covered in
muck.

So look for the colourful rainbow if you want a pot of gold,
and don't let a bird in your kitchen if you want to grow old.
Or you might want to risk it, I'm not saying that you should.
But before you make a decision, just knock three times on wood.

Gold Star.

Remember getting a gold star in school? I didn't get many as I was often far too busy daydreaming!

I'm rapidly approaching pensionable age.
I should be rather clever, a veritable sage.
But many things have passed me by; it may be now too late.
But here I'll try and have a go and set the record straight.

The periodic table, what was that all about?
They tried to teach me chemistry, but I just messed about.
The molecules collided and didn't reach my brain,
they never did quite make it through my permeable membrane.

And what about the tangents, the books full of cosines?
I didn't do my homework, but I was made to do my lines.
Isosceles triangles, the prisms and the angles,
all they did was fill my head with knotted facts and tangles.

And then there was the algebra, percentages and fractions,
I never did make sense of those or chemical reactions.
Those facts about biology, the bits that make up a cell,
all those double lessons were my idea of hell.

Physics was no better, with old Newton and his apple.
What I was going to have for lunch was more than I could grapple.
They tried to teach me Latin. Amo, Amas, Amat.
But they said I couldn't handle more than a year of that.

All I really wanted was some books by Enid Blyton,
not learning about planets and little moons called Titan.
So teachers if you read this, I've managed well so far,
even though you never gave me that coveted gold star!

The Clinic.

A more serious note here.
Please don't ignore those check up letters, they might just save your life!

A group of sombre women join up in a line.
They shuffle across the car park, hoping this time they'll be fine.
They reach a mobile clinic with steps on either side.
They register with the nurses; there is nowhere left to hide.

They step into a cubicle and strip off to the waist,
and then wait in silent anguish, knowing what they face.
They wait to be examined, breasts firmly clamped on a plate.
A nurse then takes an X ray, and the rest is left to fate.

We've heard the harsh statistics; we know that one in three
may have signs of cancer, each prays that "it's not me."
The nurses are quite cheerful, professional and kind.
They know what we are facing; they know what they may find.

These ordinary women know this may save their life.
They could be someone's daughter, a granny or a wife.
So when you get the letter, please go there for the test.
Take the screen for cancer and face it breast to breast!

Aunty Rose.

We all remember a favourite relative from our childhood. It is funny what can trigger our memories. In this case, a powdered nose!

If aunty called when we were young,
my mum would say "I wish she'd rung!"
We weren't allowed in the front room,
whilst mum raced round with mop and broom.

The table would be set just so,
our faces scrubbed and all aglow.
A tin of ham in aspic jelly,
a special treat for our young bellies.

Crusts cut off the buttered bread,
with blocks of cheese or salmon spread.
Hard boiled eggs and salad cream,
a feast of which we used to dream.

Fruit cocktail with a tin of milk,
blancmange that was as smooth as silk.
A buttered scone, a sandwich cake.
Small jam tarts that we could make.

Tea in a pot in a warm cosy,
flowers from the garden in a posy.
The posh tea cups we kept for best,
that just came out for special guests.

And we would sit as quiet as mice,
whilst aunty said the cake was nice.
We listened to the ticking clock,
in polished shoes and Sunday's frock.

Then we would ask to be excused,
we were polite and never rude.
We were allowed to read a book,
then curl up in the inglenook.

But aunty she was always kind,
and she would always leave behind,
a shiny sixpence for some sweets.
A very precious special treat.

I won't forget those childhood days,
remembered as a golden haze.
And even now a powdered nose
reminds me of my Aunty Rose!

Keys.

Dementia can strip away a person's identity. It is so important that we keep searching for the keys to their soul.

I saw a glimpse today of her.
She smiled and said, "I know you don't I?"
I smiled back.
"Yes, Mum, you know me."
The clouds had been gathering for many years.
She had brushed it off.
"It's my age; I have a mind like a sieve." We laughed.
Then we found toilet rolls in the fridge.
A phone call from the police.
They had found an elderly lady in the shopping precinct.
In her dressing gown.
In her pocket she had a photograph. It was of my dad.
We didn't want her to go into care; that was never the plan.
We tried so hard to help her stay at home.
But when she tried to light a fire in the oven, we knew.
We chose carefully. We looked for homes full of light and laughter.
We walked away from the dismal, depressing ones.
We had already lost her. Her dementia had invaded her private memories, ripping them out and discarding them like yesterday's newspapers.
Day after day she wandered the corridors, opening doors.
Looking for what she could no longer find.

We had lost her, she was gone.

But then we found a carer who told us about keys. She said dementia had slammed the doors and padlocked her hopes and dreams out of her reach.

The carer said we should all carry keys. We had to try many locks and sometimes we might never find the right one. But just when you are about to give up, one of the keys might spring the lock and we would find her again.

It may be only a glimpse, a fleeting shadow, but we would find her. Every day we tried our own keys. We brought in photographs, her favourite flowers, a childhood toy. Sometimes we would get a smile, but usually we only had the vacant look of a soul lost inside her own mind.

We had nearly run out of keys.

It was a Sunday morning. The sun was streaming in through the window and in the distance we could hear the church bells.

Mum sat gazing at the curtains. We absently-mindedly switched the radio on. Aled Jones was singing. I gazed out of the window and I was watching a blue tit picking at nuts on a bird feeder. It was then I heard a voice. I wasn't sure at first and I froze to the spot, hardly daring to breathe. She was singing, low at first but word perfect.

"All things wise and wonderful, the Lord God made them all."

I slowly turned and I saw the weight lifting from her troubled soul. Her cheeks were pink with recollection. She formed the words and sang. It was pure, sweet and perfect. We had found the key without even looking. For those few precious moments we had my mum back. The mum who went to church every Sunday and loved watching Songs of Praise. I felt a tear of joy roll down my cheek and I joined in with the familiar words. She smiled at me and when it had finished she told me to run along and tell dad dinner was ready. It was a glorious glimpse of the mum we had lost.

Look for the keys, never stop. Never give up; never stop searching, because when you find one you will be able to reach into their soul and know that they are still there.

A Plea.

It is so frustrating coming home from a day working with elderly residents, to see yet more negative press about life in a Care Home. This is a bit of a challenge to anyone who thinks we are all the same!

There are care homes on the tele
that fill us all with gloom.
With staff that are uncaring,
who lock folk in their rooms.

We look at them in horror,
it's dreadful I agree.
Abuse and filthy clothing,
we need to hear their plea.

And all my friends have seen this,
and ask me why I care.
Why work in such conditions?
I answered with a dare.

Come follow me to work one day,
and see what we all do.
It's not what you imagine,
let me change your point of view.

Don't judge us by the poor ones,
don't tar us all the same.
Don't think we all are bad guys,
that is the biggest shame.

Come see what we're achieving,
we go the extra mile.
Our job is more than cleaning,
we want to see them smile.

Our home is full of lightness,
great empathy and joy.
With carers who are vetted,
we know who to employ.

We fill their lives with purpose,
we let them make the choice.
We give them all a reason,
we let them have a voice.

We lift them up with music,
we sing their favourite songs.
It isn't always perfect,
but we know what's right or wrong.

We treat them like our parents,
always with love and respect.
We fill out all our care plans,
to ensure all things are checked.

And it isn't always easy
when we know they're at the end.
But we try and understand that,
they know they have a friend."

It's the little things that matter,
the bubbles in the bath.
The cup of tea and natter,
the chance to have a laugh.

Patience and understanding
when memories are gone,
a light that keeps them burning
and helps them carry on.

It's great to be the carer
who can change a life around.
Bring love and understanding
to one who always frowns.

So listen to the stories,
but so many homes aren't bad.
If that is your opinion,
I just feel rather sad.

But we will keep on trying
and bring bright rays of hope,
to people who are elderly
and can no longer cope.

Training Course For Carers.

If you hold all the NVQs and training courses, remember the sentiment of this short poem.

Gladys Smith. Aged 95.

This is an old lady,
hunched up in her chair.
She's crippled with arthritis,
she needs you now to care.
She's forgotten what her name is,
she stares far into space.
Your job is now to help her,
remember it's not a race.
Get down to her level,
look into her eyes.
Behind that blank expression,
is a woman who is wise.
Take her hand to guide her,
don't forget to smile.
Ask her how she's feeling,
let her take a while.
Talk about the weather,
chat about some flowers.
Try to be the difference,
in your working hours.
Do not try to rush her,

make sure that she can hear.
If she learns to trust you,
you'll take away her fear.
Don't make her decisions,
give her lots of choice.
Show her what you're doing,
let her have a voice.
Learn to spot the signals,
when she is feeling low.
The words are sometimes missing,
but you must try to know.
She may not know you've helped her
when you go out the door,
but if you've made her happy,
she'll still feel that for sure.
Learn about her hobbies,
ask about her past.
Sometimes the oldest memories,
are the ones that last.
You are not just a carer,
to her you are a raft.
Someone she can cling to,
who doesn't think she's daft.
Your job is a vocation
and you must do it right.
Never lose your patience,
never lose your sight.
Include her when you're talking,
she is somebody's mum.
Treat her like your family,

not someone deaf and dumb.
Never make a promise
that you might have to break.
Like "back in just a minute,"
this can cause so much heartache.
And never ever think that
she is just old and grey.
Remember all of your actions,
make a difference to each day.

The Change.

This is especially for women of a 'certain age'!

A woman goes through changes
when she is growing older,
her mouth forgets to button up
and she just grows much bolder.
It starts when she hits fifty
or there or thereabouts,
she starts to act quite different
and don't mention growing stout.
She used to be an angel
with patience by the bucket,
but now she doesn't care at all
and often says "oh **** it."
She suffers from hot flushes
that make her glow bright pink.
She splashes on cold water
in cupfuls from the sink.
Her mood swings like a yo yo,
from gentle, sweet and mild,
to a fiery red volcano;
(she can be very wild).
And then there are the whiskers
that start sprouting on her chin.
She plucks them out with tweezers
and throws them in the bin.

She can be quite forgetful
it's all par for the course.
But please don't say you've noticed,
she may hit you with full force.
And she might get quite sweaty
in the middle of the night,
but don't try and awake her
or she may give you a fright.
Her hair might now lack lustre
and may look rather dry,
if she asks you what you're thinking,
it might be best to lie.
And if you're feeling amorous
please approach her with great care,
because if she has a headache
she'll accept that as a dare.
But please try not to worry
it's just a passing phase,
it's only for about ten years
until you get better days!

The Well-Groomed Farmer.

Now... who could I have modelled this poem on? I wonder!

My husband went to a nail bar,
he wanted to mend his shed.
He didn't know what was happening,
when they polished him up instead.

He isn't into man grooming,
he's not done his sack or his crack.
And he'll never let anyone shave off
all the fuzz that grows on his back.

He can't see the point of a man bag,
he only has wallet and phone.
Because when he is out on his tractor
he's usually quite alone.

He laughs at the thought of a facial,
his brows aren't shaped or plucked.
He says if the salons need farmers
then their profits will probably be... marginal.

His idea of personal grooming
is a flick with a flannel and soap.
If any beauticians do spot him,
they know that he's past all hope.

He always sprays his armpits,
to counter the smell of his cows.
But he even smelt vaguely farmy,
when we exchanged our vows.

And as for fancy aromas,
perfume and eau de toilette.
He already stinks of diesel
and he's only meeting the vet.

His idea of getting a hairstyle
is me with the clippers and comb.
And even then he's still talking
to the cowman on the phone.

His hands are rough as sandpaper,
though he does use udder cream.
It stops them from cracking too badly
and it's part of his beauty regime.

But I wouldn't want to change him,
I don't like men crimped and groomed.
I'd rather have smells of cow muck,
than a man who is plucked and perfumed.

I'm happy to have my clean farmer,
even though there's a ring round the bath.
His hands are great for back rubbing
and we always have a good laugh!

Number Nineteen.

A little glimpse of farming life.

Exhaustion set in around eight o'clock. A young heifer pranced around the paddock with two tiny feet protruding from under her tail.

I was tired, grubby and hungry. I didn't need this. She appeared to be doing dressage as I attempted to corner her. The rest of the dry cows took themselves off to a feed trailer to pull on sweet, ripe silage.

Her tail swung high in the gathering gloom. She stopped to snatch at some grass, before head up, she set off again at a fast canter.

I watched her for a while from a distance. Obviously distressed, she circled and pounded at the earth.

I wanted my bed. I had anticipated finishing milking, washing down the yard, having a quick check of the cattle and going home.

It wasn't to be. The feet appeared to be upside down. I couldn't risk leaving a breech birth to nature, especially in a small heifer.

I watched as she tentatively lay down, and heard a long moan. She pushed and looked around, startled by what was happening to her. She stretched out her neck and bellowed, long and deep, before getting up and disappearing again into the gathering gloom.

My much anticipated chicken casserole, so carefully prepared earlier was probably shrivelling up as I watched, burning on to the side of the dish.

Milking had been a disaster, relatively speaking. The last heifer to calve had finally braved coming in the parlour, only to panic and with legs thrashing wildly, she had rolled into the pit with me.

I was bruised and sore by the time I had got her out and retrieved the fallen units that lay gasping and pulsing and sucking up warm slurry.

The thought of a hot meal and a warm bath had spurred me on, but number nineteen had other ideas.

I was a good two hundred yards from her when she decided to demolish the fence and crash unprovoked into the yard, skidding on her knees towards the silage pit.

At this point I was mentally querying my sanity. Why, when the rest of the world were at home, eating dinner and generally being civilised human beings, had I willingly chosen farming as a career move?

I opened the gate and let her pick her way tentatively towards it. In obvious discomfort, she snorted and picked up speed again. She launched herself at a wall and crashed down on her side. This was my chance. A little pressure on the feet and she resigned herself to her fate. There was no chance of the niceties, gloves, warm water, and a calf puller. Just me and a bottle of lube, a scared animal and a potential vet's bill to consider.

I maintained the pressure on the legs which immobilised her and she rested her head on the concrete floor, eyes rolling. A feeble attempt at moving and she lay back again. I worked quickly. I attached the ropes that I had retrieved from my pockets and feeling the calf's tail, I pulled down. This time she helped me. Her back legs thrashed the air and then she pushed. The wet calf came out at speed and lay lifeless on the floor. The heifer lay still, panting, oblivious to what had just happened.

I cleared the mucous from the calf's nostrils and mouth. I had precious little time to save it, if save it I could. I massaged its leg on to its chest and tickled its nose with straw. For a whole minute, there was no response. Then suddenly and explosively it sneezed. Shaking its wobbly head it blinked and surveyed its new world. I dragged it to the front of the heifer. She looked shocked, then made a primeval bellow and instinctively started licking it with her raspy tongue. I breathed a sigh of relief. The calf mooed and the heifer responded with a low throaty call. I stepped back and proudly took in the scene under the harsh yard light. Nature had taken control and number nineteen's innate senses had finally kicked in. In that precious moment I realised that I actually had the best job in the world, even if dinner was now likely to be a cheese sandwich and a bag of crisps.

Wimbledon.

For two glorious weeks in June we get a reason to relax with a cold drink and some strawberries and cream, whilst enjoying the wonderful spectacle that is Wimbledon.

Two weeks of tennis every June.
Some moan and groan,
others will cry.
Roof on, roof off.
Change the balls.
Thirty, forty, on the line calls.
Advantage, match point,
jingly nerves.
Double faults and
powerful serves.
Broken rackets,
tempers lost.
Strawberries and cream,
(ignore the cost).
Umpires, hawk eye,
in and out.
Some will sulk,
others pout.
Centre court crowds,
fine mown grass.
A special box
for the upper class.

Headbands, caps,
tight white skirts.
Titanium rackets,
Fred Perry shirts.
Back hands, rallies,
covers on courts.
Rain stops play,
new brollies bought.
Towels for wiping
a sweating face,
bottles of squash
to help the pace.
Doubles, singles,
fairy tale endings.
Attacking nets and
desperate defending.
Autograph hunters
looking for the stars.
Drinking Pimms
in trendy bars.
Plaited ball girls
on the run.
Matches lost,
trophies won.
Line judges stoop
to watch the line.
Grey cloudy skies
and then it's fine.
Murray's Mound
or Henman's Hill.

Thousands watch,
it's such a thrill.
Ladies' finals,
smiles and tears.
Plates held high,
lots of cheers.
Then the men
fight for their cup.
They may be tired,
but they step up.
Now it's all over,
the days have flown.
New stars shine,
fresh seeds are sown.
Purple and green,
the Wimbledon colours.
Watching in the stand,
proud fathers and mothers.
Wimbledon means
summer has begun.
We've loved every minute
when all's said and done!

Budget Airways.

As summer holidays to exotic places loom, we prepare ourselves for negotiating the airport terminal!

We're going on a holiday, we booked it last September.
We're flying Budget Airways, we hope that they remember.
We've booked two seats behind the wing, it's safer there you see.
So if we have to get out quick, the exit's right by me.

We turned up at the airport, three hours before the flight.
We had to have our bags packed in the middle of the night.
We parked our car in aisle ten, blue zone, ninety-four.
We had to go back twice to check that we'd locked the door.

We heaved our cases on the bus that shuttles round the cars.
We had to stand and hang on tight to yellow coloured bars.
We're pushed and shoved and rolled around at terrifying speed,
with our face against a poster that says comfort's guaranteed.

We rolled up at the terminal and shuddered to a halt.
But the doors then failed to open, there seemed to be a fault.
The driver got quite stroppy and rolled out of his cab,
and with a large screwdriver, gave the doors a frightening jab.

We poured on to the concrete, with suitcases in tow.
Handles all retracted, we are dragged on by the flow.
We are faced with rows of check in gates to places far away.
We searched to find the one that's ours, we didn't have all day.

With queues of anxious people all wanting to check in,
winding round a maze of ropes, to Oslo or Berlin.
Pushing on their cases, shuffling slowly in a line,
hoping that they'll make it through and not run out of time.

We found our Budget Airways was running one hour late.
But we had to check our luggage in, so we settled in to wait.
It took us forty minutes until it finally was our turn.
We rummaged for our passports, the lady looked quite stern.

She asked if we had packed our bags or left them unattended.
(If she was friends on Facebook, I think she'd be unfriended).
She eyed us up like criminals standing quietly in the dock,
and checked our zips and labels, not caring for the clock.

We put the cases on the track so she could check their weight.
The numbers were all flashing up at an alarming rate.
We passed the test and off they went to load up on our plane,
first thrown with gay abandon to a passing luggage train.

We then head for departures with boarding cards in hand,
security is waiting to check for all that's banned.
We drink up all the water, take off our coats and shoes.
They have the right to search you, so either way you lose.

We watched with fascination as some left for Alicante.
A group of noisy youngsters in clothes all bright and scanty.
And then the ones for Zurich dressed up for lots of snow.
Sweating in their jumpers, with faces all aglow.

When finally it was our turn we queued again to board.
You get on first with fast track, but not many can afford.
But they won't get there faster, they have to wait for us.
I can't see why they do it, it's never worth the fuss.

And now we are excited because our holiday's begun.
Seven days of sunshine, seven days of fun.
And when it is all over we'll get back in the queue,
then check our Trip Advisor and send off a nice review.

Dad.

He's always there, just out of sight. In the corners of my mind.

My dad he was my hero,
he also carried sweets.
He always used to buy me,
special little treats.

He always smelled of Brylcreem,
which he combed into his hair.
He puffed pipes of tobacco
and never had a care.

It was dad who gave me money,
when I was running low.
I only had to ask him,
now it seems so long ago.

I found he had some medals,
from when he was in the war.
He kept them in a tin box,
behind a cupboard door.

He taught me how to care for
creatures great and small,
but I got into trouble
when I took lambs into our hall.

And if I had been naughty,
my mum would say to me,
"Just wait until your dad gets home,
after he's had his tea."

But he never got too angry,
he would just give me a look,
over his old spectacles,
above his favourite book.

There was something just so special,
about my dear old dad.
Now sometimes I feel happy,
and sometimes I am sad.

I'll miss him for forever
and there and back again.
He was so very special
and life isn't quite the same.

But as I now remember,
I realise I was blessed.
I hope that he is peaceful,
in his eternal rest.

Mum.

It is very hard to care for an elderly parent and see them deteriorate and change. This poem is for anyone walking this pathway. Hang in there; you can only do your best.

When I was just a little girl,
before my life had then unfurled,
my mother did the best for me,
she gave me wings to set me free.

She wiped my face, she dried my tears.
She taught me how to face my fears.
She showed me how to be the best,
I knew that I was truly blessed.

And now she faces her worst fears.
She can't remember all those years
of love and laughter, pain and smiles.
Now empty space for miles and miles.

It hurts to see her, just a shell.
And we must face the long farewell.
We see her fade before our eyes.
That sad old face, a thin disguise.

But every now and then I see,
the woman that she used to be.
So generous, kind and funny.
Making every day seem sunny.

And I will hang on to the end,
although her mind I cannot mend.
I know she loves me deep inside,
all I can do is know I've tried.

So Mother I will not forget.
I'll hold your hand so you won't fret.
I'll try and show you how I care,
I'll stand by you, though you're not there.

And many days will be so hard,
the things you say may leave me scarred.
But love is deeper, love is kind.
Our lives will always be entwined.

And when we say our last goodbye,
when finally you're free to fly.
I hope you know that I was there,
and in the darkness heard my prayer.

The Old House.

Memories are precious and sometimes we have to let go and move on, but once in a while we should pause our busy lives and remember.

I held the door and paused, absorbing the memories. The creaking door in the bathroom. The burn on the skirting board from a dropped iron. Pencil marks on the utility wall marking forgotten growth spurts of children and grandchildren.

The sink, unusually empty, was where we had washed a thousand dishes and wiped away dirt from a myriad of muddied knees and faces.

The ugly stain on the carpet where the contents of a bottle of wine had spilled its crimson contents one Christmas looked exposed.

A glorious tangle of forgotten memories lay cemented into the very fabric of the place.

We left the curtains, deep brick red, but faded where they had met the sun on countless mornings. They had provided grateful protection from icy draughts that had somehow seeped under the ancient frames on cold, dark, winter nights.

A line on the carpet marked the spot where the Welsh dresser had stood proud and imposing against the dining room wall. The familiar willow pattern dinner set which had adorned its polished oak shelves for over fifty years, was now carefully wrapped, bound for a new home. A ticket from a long forgotten bus trip lay curled forlornly in a corner.

A dripping tap echoed in the stillness.

The hull remained. The flotsam and jetsam of life bundled into packing boxes. Precious ornaments had been gently wrapped in brown paper and labelled fragile.

Dusty cobwebs hung where the Victorian wardrobe had dominated the bedroom. It had proved too large for us to move, but was eventually carried away by burly removal men, who cursed and sweated as they heaved its dusty carcass down the narrow staircase.

The silence weighed heavy. No familiar clock to mark down the unforgiving seconds of life, whirring and groaning. Fighting against each passing hour.

The rose that we had bought them for their wedding anniversary had brushed against the window as we surveyed the scene. We were desperately trying to cram every familiar corner of this old life into our heads before it was gone and out of reach.

Another tear shed, another life gone, another story confined to memory. I took in the creaky third stair, carefully avoided by teenagers returning too late at night. The fireplace with the cracked tile, once carefully concealed by a polished copper kettle, now exposed and ugly.

The door had seen so many changes, happy arrivals and desperately sad departures, with the old familiar key worn from generations of use. It was now set to shut on this past life forever.

The new owners would strip it back, expose forgotten beams, splash colourful paint over the layers of wood chip. They would fill the rooms with joy and laughter. The bathroom door would swing fixed and silent, all vestiges of our old family life removed. The house would surely remember the joy and rejoice with the vibrant new youngsters that were exploring its secret nooks and crannies. But when the wind blows from the west when the summer is nearly over, that old red rose, replanted outside our kitchen may catch the breeze and scatter scarlet petals on our window sill and we will smile and remember.

A day in the life of an Activity Coordinator.

A little glimpse into the gloriously varied life of my job as an Activity Coordinator in a Care Home!

Paper flowers made in bright colours,
cups of tea to involve others.
Painting pots in every hue,
sticking stuff with roll on glue.

Having fun with new found friends,
making crafts from odds and ends.
Winding wool and knitting squares,
comfy blankets for the chairs.

Collages from leaves and shells,
reminiscing about smells.
Planting bulbs in pretty bowls,
having fun is our main goal.

Rolling pastry, making tarts.
Giving all a chance to start.
Peeling carrots, shelling peas.
Grating up big blocks of cheese.

Folding napkins, pairing socks.
Brightly splashing, painting rocks.
Daisies made from scraps of card,
bird cakes mixed with seeds and lard.

Beads and buttons, stick on eyes.
Birds and paper butterflies.
Flower arranging in little jars,
stickers, shapes and little stars.

Sandpaper for blocks of wood,
say you can, not just you could.
Have a go and be the spark,
make a joke and have a lark.

Proverbs, quizzes, daily news.
Listening to others' views.
Jigsaws, games and guess the song.
There is no right, there is no wrong.

Singing songs from way back when,
doodling with a coloured pen.
Poetry we learned at school,
home-made cakes to make us drool.

Boxes full for all to treasure,
sorting necklaces at leisure.
Books and magazines galore,
always time for something more.

Games of cards with silly prizes.
Hats in funny shapes and sizes.
Bingo, Boccia, name that tune,
mobiles hung in every room.

Hymns and songs for us to choose,
airy rooms in which to snooze.
Bells and drums and home-made shakers,
discussions from the daily papers.

Planting beans and tending roses,
picking and choosing floral posies.
Getting out for fish and chips,
exercising dodgy hips.

Cats and dogs around us roam,
they too have made this place their home.
Lots of laughter, time for sherry.
There's nothing wrong with being merry!

One Job.

Remember when life was simple? When paint was either matt or gloss and there was a choice of about six colours? All I wanted was a pot of magnolia.

I drive up to my local store,
I need to paint the hall.
It is starting to look grubby,
there are paw prints up the wall.

I want some plain magnolia,
I just want it to look nice.
I want a one coat product,
I don't want to do it twice.

I'm confronted with vast alleyways
of paints in every hue.
I can't find my magnolia,
I don't know what to do.

There is honey pot and chiffon,
vanilla pie and shimmer.
Desert sand and gossamer,
if you want it slightly dimmer.

There's tiger's sneeze and calico,
Hessian grey and stone.
Mocha, Spanish pebbles,
Dorset ice cream cone.

There's Jersey milk and shadow,
soured beer and truffle.
Biscuit crunch and pewter steel,
(this is a great kerfuffle).

I could opt for wispy oyster,
or stick with boring white.
The sumptuous pout or coral twist
might give my dogs a fright.

I think I like spring blossom,
whipped drizzle and crushed rose.
Luscious cream and candy floss,
I could choose one of those.

But then there's sunshine ripple,
harvest moon and puddle.
Why do they have so much choice?
I'm a multicoloured muddle.

I'm not sure if sweet walnut
is darker than burnt feather.
If macaroon is overcooked,
will it look like dirty leather?

I go home quite exhausted,
I think I'll just use bleach.
Then move the aspidistra,
so the wall is out of reach!

Parking.

Parking in town can be a real trial. I am beginning to think I am town intolerant!

I think I'm town intolerant,
I cannot cope with shopping.
I don't mind driving through them,
the problem is with stopping.

I need to go in sometimes
for a gift or some new shoes,
but I have trouble looking,
there's far too much to choose.

I drive to the multistorey
and I circle like a shark,
waiting for a shopper
to leave me space to park.

I spot a lady with a trolley
loading up her boot,
she's starting up her engine
and I'm in hot pursuit.

But a woman in a Mini,
has spotted her as well.
We both rev' up our engines,
we're on the road to hell.

Then an old man in an Escort
sneaks in the space behind.
He gets out with a white stick,
(I think he may be blind).

I feel the pressure mounting,
my patience is wearing thin.
And then I see a free bay,
I'll fit if I breathe in.

I walk up to the meter,
two pounds for just two hours.
It's really not surprising,
everyone looks so sour.

I rummage in my handbag,
I search beneath my seats.
I see the park attendant
pounding up the street.

I've scraped my cash together,
I think I've got it right.
I stick it in the meter,
but then I get a fright.

It tells me I have only
one pound and seventy-five.
I need to find more money,
or use the park and drive.

I feel the queue behind me,
I hear the tuts and sighs.
But then nestled in my pocket
I find the perfect prize.

A hidden little treasure,
a coin just what I need.
I stick it in the meter,
that monster we all feed.

But it's eaten all my money
and I haven't got a ticket.
I'm very close to crying,
this really isn't cricket.

I stomp back to my parked car,
in my mind I'm seeing red.
I'll go shopping on the internet
without getting out of bed.

And as I start my engine
I can feel those watching eyes.
All eyeing up my parking space,
all driving round clockwise.

I know I'm town intolerant,
I prefer to stay at home.
I shall order stuff from Amazon,
or on the telephone.

But if you see me driving
and looking for a space.
Please signal if you're leaving
and let me take your place!

Glastonbury.

I live a few miles from Glastonbury and watching the annual music festival on TV, it so often becomes a mud bath. I must admit that I much prefer my home comforts!

I could be an attendant
and be in charge of loos.
Cleaning up at Glastonbury
with toilets full of poos.

It really makes me shudder,
it truly must be grim.
Tackling all those cubicles
filled right up to the brim.

And I feel very grateful,
I thank my lucky stars.
That I'm not stuck in traffic,
in miles and miles of cars.

I can live without the music,
I must be getting old.
I couldn't cope with camping,
I'd be muddy and quite cold.

Adele I find depressing,
she just keeps going on,
about her old boyfriends,
she never can move on.

Coldplay they'll be singing
about their paradise,
with thousands in their wellies,
it's not my idea of nice.

I hope they all enjoy it
but it's my idea of hell.
I'm not too good with people,
the noises and the smell.

So all you folk out camping
in fields all over Pylle.
Having wet wipe washes
and feeling rather ill.

I hope you do enjoy it,
you can say that you were there.
But I am more than happy
sat at home in my own chair.

Car.

I am starting to sound like a real killjoy, but I really don't care what sort of car I drive. As long as it starts!

I don't need a car that is shiny,
I don't care if it's purple or white.
I just want to be able to drive it,
if I want to get home safe at night.

I don't care for alloy suspension,
I don't want to have cruise control.
All I need is a reliable engine,
and four tyres that hopefully roll.

I don't worry about folding up mirrors,
or if it can connect to blue tooth.
I much prefer to have steering,
doors and a nice solid roof.

The salesman gives me his patter,
he thinks that I am impressed.
But I don't need sat' navigation
and I wish he'd give it a rest.

I still use my trusty old map book
that gets me from A to Z,
as long as I set my alarm clock
and heave myself out of my bed.

I yearn for the days that were easy
when I checked my own points and plugs.
Kept a spare pair of tights with the spanners,
and covered my knees with a rug.

I used to wind down the window
and pull out the choke to get going.
Put a weight in the boot if it was icy,
and a shovel and flask when snowing.

But now it's all on computers,
we don't even get our hands dirty.
If you ask the garage for answers,
they sometimes get a bit shirty.

And whatever happened to bumpers?
They saved quite a few dents and tears.
And remember how life was so easy
with reverse and four simple gears?

Cars are getting quite boring,
to me they look much the same.
And now if you have an accident,
everyone's out for a claim.

Some have to buy fancy new motors
designed for high fashion and speed,
with a hundred expensive new extras
that none of us really will need.

Because dreams of cruising the highways
like the adverts they show on TV,
are more likely to be more of a nightmare,
where you're stuck in a queue and can't pee!

Aberfan.

The disaster in Aberfan where so many lives were lost was one of the darkest days in Welsh history. I wrote this poem after watching a very moving documentary on the TV.

The mist hung low that morning,
that fateful autumn day.
The school was full of children,
ready to work and play.

No one saw it coming,
though some heard a mighty roar.
A hundred thousand tons of shale,
slid down the valley floor.

So many young lives buried,
as families searched in vain.
The whole town stood there weeping,
amidst the cloud and rain.

Since then we all remember
the town called Aberfan.
The tragic line of coffins,
lives gone as they began.

So many prayers unanswered,
mud moved with raw bare hands.
No one could give them solace,
no one could understand.

The stories will live forever
of the families torn apart.
A hundred thousand tear drops,
from every broken heart.

9/11.

An ordinary day which was turned into a grotesque scene, forever forged in our memories as one of the bleakest of days in world history.

It was the eleventh of September
a clear blue autumn sky.
Folk gathered at the airports,
not knowing they would die.

People having breakfast,
preparing for their day.
Traffic busy queuing
along the state highway.

Firemen at the stations
waiting for a call.
Policemen out patrolling
busy shopping malls.

Then chaos in the city,
murder in the sky.
A plane hits the first tower,
and no one knows just why.

Confusion turns to panic,
then another does the same.
The world turns on its axis,
we don't know who to blame.

The president gets the message,
he says we are at war.
But we don't know who we're fighting,
or who we're looking for.

People trapped above us,
some fall down like rain.
The whole world is in crisis,
so many watch their pain.

We watch the news with terror
as the damage now unfolds.
Dark clouds hang o'er the city,
our blood has all run cold.

So many died as heroes,
too many lives were lost.
Unfathomable damage,
we can never count the cost.

And now we must remember
and each one of us must try
to be good to one another,
look back and hear their cry.

We must face this world of hatred
and recall that fateful day.
Replace the hurt with kindness
and wipe bitter tears away.

One Hundred Years.

2016 marked the 100th anniversary of the battle of the Somme. We must never forget their sacrifice.

One hundred years ago this year in trenches across France,
a hundred thousand soldiers who never stood a chance.
They signed up for their country; they joined up for their King,
but they would be the sacrifice, death would have its sting.

That khaki clad army, some were only just sixteen.
They didn't see it coming, the carnage was unseen.
And then that fateful morning with a whistle loud and shrill,
they poured out of the trenches, they were sent out there to kill.

And as the clouds were lifting on the first day of July,
nineteen thousand soldiers were destined there to die.
They ran into machine guns, mown down into the mud.
Their brave young faces silent, covered now in blood.

Each one of the white gravestones hides a gallant heart.
Too many lives were wasted, too many torn apart.
And so we must remember that war to end all wars.
The flowers of a nation, what were they fighting for?

They gave their lives in battle, they wanted to be free.
But many lie there buried in fields across the sea.
A hundred years have passed now; no one is left to tell.
We must still remember that for us they went through hell.

So when you eat your cornflakes and face the bright new day,
just pause for a few minutes and think of them and pray.
For us they gave their future, so many brave young men.
We see the faded photo's, we won't see their like again.

The Old Soldier.

Many of the residents that I have cared for have been war veterans. They are the generation who were expected to just 'get on with it'. It is something all carers should remember when trying to understand behaviour.

He lies in his bed staring at the wall,
if he tries to stand he knows that he may fall.
He listens for the carers, the ticking of the clock.
Behind his own door that doesn't have a lock.

The carers come in and roll him on his bed,
they wash and clean him and make sure he is fed.
They all are kind but he is just a shell,
they spray the room to cover up the smell.

Day after day, he knows the same routine.
Fridays it's a shower, they like to keep him clean.
They shave his face but don't look into his eyes,
or see the man behind his frail disguise.

He hears the sound of the medicine cart,
a nurse comes in and fills out his chart.
She gives him a pill and walks out of the door.
Just another patient, just another chore.

The TV is on, he hasn't got a choice.
He wants to rest but doesn't have a voice.
He knows he is there waiting just to die,
praying for the angels to show him how to fly.

He closes his eyes and recalls his life,
if only he still had his beautiful wife.
She could make him laugh, she could make him sing.
She would turn his winter back into a spring.

He hears the sound of distant guns,
he starts to scream until a carer runs.
She tries to calm him, but he is back at war.
He cannot forget what they had all died for.

The sun goes down and he still feels pain,
he rings his bell again and again.
But he cannot convey the words won't come out.
The carers tell him it's not good to shout.

Here lies a soldier, who did his part.
Here lies a hero with a broken old heart.
Here lies a person in need of respect,
here is a person desperate to connect.

Look past the old man curled up in a ball,
put up some pictures on that bare white wall.
Give him back his dignity, throw him out a rope.
Be a ray of sunshine when he cannot cope.

The carers are busy and sometimes forget to see
this person who fought, so we could all be free.
He is an old soldier, the war it may be won.
But his final battle has only just begun.

Food for free!

I grew up in the country and I love filling my store cupboard with 'food for free'!

I've raspberries in the garden,
damsons on my tree.
Blackberries in the hedgerow,
I love the food that's free!

There are mushrooms in the meadow,
sweet chestnuts in the wood.
If you roast them in hot cinders,
they taste so blooming good.

A neighbour leaves tomatoes
in a bag outside the door,
with a note just to remind me
to ask if I want more.

I give eggs laid by my chickens,
in return I get green beans.
Courgettes and bright red peppers,
a feast fit for a Queen.

I have jam in shining jam jars,
all rowed up on a ledge.
Made from fruit that I've discovered
growing wild along a hedge.

I have chutney made from apples,
from the orchard out the back.
I went to pick a couple,
and came back with a full sack.

And then there are the marrows,
we get those by the ton.
If you let on that you like them,
you'll never get just one!

I love the herbs just waiting
to be made into a sauce.
Rosemary and mint will
go with lamb of course!

Parsley by the handful,
sage and bay leaves too.
Thyme will wait for no man,
so don't just pick a few.

And there is something special
about picking food yourself,
so much better for you
than from a supermarket shelf.

A bit of local barter
and you can fill your store,
with local fresh grown produce,
who could want for more?

The Art Of Dyeing.

Dyeing can be a very satisfying experience!

My life has been quite normal,
boring some might say.
I've been to school and college,
and went to church to pray.

I started work at twenty
and worked my way on through.
Although I didn't like it much,
it was something we all do.

I've had some happy holidays
and married my first love.
We have the perfect cottage,
and a car we are proud of.

Our garden has some roses
that grow back every year,
and we planted some asparagus,
and some apples and a pear.

We have two perfect children,
who grew up just like us.
They didn't want for money,
and they never made a fuss.

But I have now been thinking
now life is getting on,
I don't want it all to finish
without a bit of fun.

So I've spoken to my family
and told them I am dyeing.
I wasn't well prepared for it
when they all started crying.

They looked a little worried
so I took them to one side,
until they finally noticed
the bright clothes that I had dyed!

Winter In A Care Home.

Care homes are always very warm. You may turn up at work in coat and cardigan, but you will soon strip off to shirt sleeves regardless of the time of year!

The heating went on in August,
there are blankets on every knee.
A constant demand for hot chocolate,
radiators notched up a degree.

Hot bottles of water are needed,
to warm up fingers and toes.
Blankets are got out of cupboards,
everyone's wrapped up in throws.

Winter is coming quite quickly,
frost is covering the lawn.
But all our bedrooms are boiling
and we try to stifle a yawn.

Someone comes in from the garden
and lets in an icy cold blast,
which causes old Fred to shout out:
"Make sure you shut that door fast!"

But winter can be sometimes special,
we can watch the birds on the grass.
It may be grey and dull weather,
but we know one day it will pass.

We talk of winters now long gone,
when we had to shovel the path,
then heat up pans full of water
just so we could have a hot bath.

We remember the blizzards and snowdrifts
when we couldn't get out of the door.
When the windows had frost on the inside,
in the years just after the war.

There's something about being cosy
when the weather is bitter outside,
with a bowl of soup and some knitting
snuggled up by a glowing fireside .

Then there's the run up to Christmas,
with lots of goodies to make.
Hyacinth bowls planted ready,
sweet tasty mince pies to bake.

And then there are programmes on tele',
which come round at this time of year.
Panto's and shows in abundance,
to keep us all in good cheer.

It's great to look at the weather
when you are as snug as a bug.
Having a sip of sweet sherry,
or something hot in a mug.

And winter brings us a promise
that there'll always be a new spring.
So snuggle up and enjoy it
and enjoy the gifts that it brings!

The Power Of Music.

Music is a powerful tool that can unlock forgotten memories and bring so much pleasure.

A little rhyme that you first learned whilst on your mother's knee.
A verse or two from Sunday school sung loud and out of key.
A poem chanted whilst you skipped with friends so long ago,
all have the power to take you back, it's something you must know.

Stored in the back room of your brain just waiting to unlock,
an orchestra of memories to turn back the ticking clock.
The songs you heard when you were young stay with you all your life,
and bring the good times flooding back and take away your strife.

The hymns you sung whilst still at school can calm you while you sleep.
The songs you used to dance to are the melodies that you'll keep.
Music can break down barriers and reach into a troubled mind,
it calms the soul and brings a smile and leaves the cares behind.

The first notes sound familiar and soon the words will come.
They're etched so deep within your soul that you will start to hum.
And waves of well-known rhythms will fill your heart with pleasure,
the soundtracks to your lifetime are the ones to always treasure.

Let music be the rhythm that guides you home again.
Let it soar beyond the storm clouds that gather in the brain.
Let the notes cascade like diamonds and scatter in the sun,
then unite your mind with purpose and fill your life with fun!

Christmas Parking.

I always try and not leave it until the last minute, but Christmas has a tendency to creep up on us when we are not looking!

Slowly moves the queue of traffic
heading for the Christmas shops.
When you think that things are moving,
just as quickly all things stop.

Signs outside the multistorey,
highlighted in bright red lights.
Show there are no empty spaces,
no room in there for us tonight.

Round and round the city car parks,
prowling like a hungry bear.
Waiting for someone to go home,
answering our hopeful prayer.

Then we see a man returning,
loaded up with bags and beer.
Filling up his car with presents,
to give others Christmas cheer.

We wait for him to start his engine,
whilst those behind us honk their horns.
Everyone is getting stressful,
patience is thin and very worn.

The man decides that he's not finished
and gets back out to get some more.
We drive on by and in the mirror,
he's heading back to his car door.

And then at last we get lucky
and park the car a mile away.
At least it's cheap for late night shoppers.
Now we're here, we're going to stay.

Fifteen shops and we're still going,
bags stuffed full of thoughtful gifts.
Woolly slippers for great granny,
another off the shopping list.

Finally the shops are shutting,
our feet are sore and very tired.
But we've forgotten where the car is
and the ticket has expired.

We see the dreaded traffic warden
just behind where we are parked.
He is busy writing tickets,
we hope it's not our card he's marked.

We scuttle past and throw our bags in,
put on our belts and drive away.
We wave and shout out "Merry Christmas"
and live to shop another day!

Christmas On The Farm.

Many of us have to work over Christmas and that certainly includes farmers!

It may be Christmas morning,
but we can't have a day off.
The cows are in for milking,
they need cow cake in their trough.

The dogs are looking hopeful,
they want to have a run.
Opening Christmas presents
isn't their idea of fun.

The cowman has put tinsel
around the dairy door,
it is sparkling and reflecting
on the muck upon the floor.

The wind is blowing briskly
around the stack of bales,
the rain is cold and slowly
turning into frozen hail.

The cows are steaming nicely,
chewing on their cud.
The cowman's got his wellies,
stuck firmly in the mud.

The village lights are twinkling
as they wake on Christmas Day,
whilst the farmers are unwrapping
great bales of straw and hay.

The calves have started bawling,
expecting to be fed,
whilst others are all cosy,
opening presents in their bed.

But when you've finished milking
and made sure that all is well.
And taken off your wellies,
and washed away the smell.

You'll walk into a warm kitchen,
thaw out your sore, tired hands.
Knowing that all your family
will love and understand.

Undertaking.

Please don't!

If you're behind a tractor
with an indicator on.
It probably means he's turning,
so please wait until he's gone.

Please use a bit of patience,
it's really not a race.
He needs some room to get there,
so back off and give him space.

If you try and undertake him
you might find it's you in need,
of a firm of undertakers,
however fast your speed.

Please use a bit of common
and by that I do mean sense,
or you could find you're squashed up
between a trailer and a fence.

Christmas.

Does this sound familiar?

Halloween has come and gone.
The clocks are back, the heating's on.
The weather's gloomy, fog and mist.
The kids prepare their Santa list.

The shops are decked with spray on snow.
The trees are up, all systems go.
The supermarkets pack their shelves
with fresh mince pies and chocolate elves.

Carols speak of peace on earth.
There's little sign of a holy birth.
Aled Jones floats in the air,
in every hall, at every fair.

Men are looking quite harassed,
buying stuff to go in baths.
Checking labels, guessing sizes,
hoping for some nice surprises.

Books on cooking, fishing, knitting.
Shoppers on the verge of quitting.
Festive jumpers, knitted scarves.
Silly presents just for laughs.

Wreaths of holly, Christmas trees.
Woolly hats against the freeze.
Queues of shoppers getting stressed,
part time staff that try their best.

Santa's grotto, tacky toys.
Dolls for girls and balls for boys.
Tinsel, paper, rolls of tape,
parcels wrapped in every shape.

Credit cards to pay the bills,
hot mulled wine against the chills.
Sally Army sing out clear,
filling us with Christmas cheer.

Presents hidden under beds,
tables groan with festive spreads.
Lights adorn each festive street,
orders made for joints of meat.

Plastic snowflakes, paper chains.
Prayers for snow, but it just rains.
Angel costumes, tiny Kings.
Turtle doves and five gold rings.

Finally the shops are shut.
We've too much food, we have a glut.
Parcels arrive from Amazon,
last posting date has been and gone.

The kids wake up at five am,
we try and send them back again.
But we know they are so excited,
there is no point in trying to fight it.

We stop to watch the Queen's speech,
the remote control is out of reach.
Turkeys cook around the land,
aunts and uncles lend a hand.

Gran has drunk a lot of sherry.
Her face is pink, she's very merry.
We're all full of Christmas cheer,
Mum's on the gin, Dad's got a beer.

The shops will soon be full of sales,
with reindeer suits displayed on rails.
And we all say we'll join the gym
and sausage rolls will be a sin!

The Village Gossip.

Be very careful what you say, because by the time it gets back to you it may be very different indeed!

Mrs Sylvia Smith was telling Melanie Morris about her husband's bunion.

This was misheard by Jennifer Jones, who thought she had halitosis from eating onions. Her neighbour Stephanie Butler took it that bad breath was having a negative effect on Sylvia's marriage to George. Stephanie told her hairdresser Pippa, who told Monica Adkins, but Monica was under the drier and thought she was talking about Sheila Carter. Sheila was the local chiropodist and had been booked for a private visit by Sylvia for a professional opinion. When Sheila was seen chatting to George in the supermarket by the grapefruit, Brenda Hopkins reported to Ethel Bennett that she heard Sheila call him sweet, whereas she had been talking about his feet. Ethel reported the liaison to Shirley Harptree, the church organist at choir practice and she promised to pray for her soul, but not before telling Tina Green that Ethel had feelings for George, because why else would she be trying to come between a husband and his wife?

Tina quickly booked herself in for a perm so that she could see the look on Pippa's face when she found out that Ethel had been sleeping with George, but was she horrified to see George in the chair having a dry trim. Pippa was being particularly attentive and when George told her he was going away on business, she naturally assumed that he was in fact booking a hotel for a sordid romp with Shirley, because why else would Shirley have her roots done two weeks before she was due? This was witnessed by Danielle Baker who decided to inform Angela Atkinson from The Nags Head that Pippa had been rather frivolous with George and wondered if Pippa's Barry knew quite how flirtatious she was at work. She decided to ask Emma Butcher if she knew that Pippa was sexually attracted to Sylvia's George. Emma said she had noticed an attraction, but didn't think anything of it, although Barry had been cutting the hedge next door to Sylvia's garden with his shirt off, which was obviously a blatant signal that he knew all about the affair and was flaunting himself in a vain attempt at revenge.

Melanie Morris walked into the hairdressers and reaching in her handbag, she handed George 'Special cream and a dressing', which caused Pippa to drop her scissors. George, in a rare moment of pleasure, glimpsed Pippa's breasts as she stooped to pick the scissors up off the floor, just as Sylvia walked past the window. Sylvia stormed in the salon and grabbing poor George by the ear marched him home on his bad bunion. Barry was at that moment eating home-made flapjack given to him by Shirley, who just happened to be passing, (although she still had her binoculars hung around her neck).

That night George made passionate love to his surprised wife whilst imagining the tantalising glimpse of Pippa's ample bosom. Barry had developed a nasty rash from leaving his shirt off on such a hot day and was sleeping in the spare room so as not to interfere with Tina's new tan. The rest of the village rested ready for a new day tomorrow.

Thanks.

Thanks to all the people
I've met along life's track.
The ones who helped me growing,
the ones who watched my back.

The teachers who endured me
as I struggled on through school.
The one who tried to help me,
though I'd broken every rule.

The boys and girls who teased me
for not being quite the same.
They never ever picked me
to play in any game.

The bullies when they tripped me
and laughed and called me names.
They all have made me stronger,
I don't hold them to blame.

The one who said he loved me
who gave me my first kiss.
He broke my heart in pieces,
but I had to go through this.

My mum, my dad and sister,
the constants in my life.
The man I gave my heart to
when I became his wife.

The boss who saw potential
and gave me a precious chance.
The loyal friends and lovers
who taught me how to dance.

The people I have worked with.
The laughs, the threats, the tears.
The ones who showed me how to
face up to all my fears.

Each one has had an impact
and some have left deep scars.
But thanks to all the good guys
who have pointed out the stars!

I Am.

We are all just another member of the human race, regardless of our opinions, appearance and beliefs.

I'm a white American
born in the USA.
I'm a black South African,
I'm a straight guy and a gay.

I'm an Afghan rebel
fighting for a cause.
I'm an English vicar,
praying to stop wars.

I'm a Muslim woman,
beneath a sacred veil.
I'm a young man, I'm a pensioner.
I am strong and I am frail.

I'm a tough Australian,
rounding up my sheep.
I'm a widowed lady,
trying not to weep.

I'm a brave young soldier
but I don't want to die.
I'm a lonely spinster
and I'm a Russian spy.

I'm a Chinese farmer
working on the land.
I'm an Arab businessman
in deserts full of sand.

I'm a part of history
waiting to unfold.
I'm a poor prospector
hoping to strike gold.

I'm a living being
with blood the same as you.
I shall never challenge
or change your point of view.

I have skin that's yellow,
black or palest white.
I pray for our future,
in the darkest night.

I am just another
part of all mankind,
I see all our problems,
but I know that I'm blind.

I can make a difference,
I'm too poor to care.
I have many riches,
I don't think it's fair.

I hope that when you read this,
the message is quite clear.
If you see past the prejudice
we'll have nothing left to fear.

Remember.

November is the month of remembrance.

Today's the time for us to remember,
on this cold day, the 11th November.
We think back on the folk we've lost,
as winter turns the fields to frost.

First we must recall the Somme,
one hundred years have come and gone.
Those brave young men who went to war,
it was our freedom they fought for.

And we recall the souls who've gone.
Beyond the sky, to light the sun.
Our friends and family that have left,
and we can sometimes feel bereft.

Now life goes on, the seasons change.
Without their voice it can seem strange.
Their lives we praise, their time had come,
they wouldn't want us always glum.

Together we'll think of them today,
we'll sing some songs and kneel and pray.
We're thankful that we had the chance,
to share their path, to watch them dance.

Lift up your voice, sing out their song.
To smile and laugh is never wrong.
Look to the sky and see them shine,
and raise a glass for auld lang syne.

Saving Mrs Smith.

Never underestimate anyone!

The bull has got out and has gone down the road.
His nose is right up, he's in escape mode.
The postie has cleared an old five barred gate.
His letters are scattered, he looks in a state.

And old Mrs Smith is out there collecting wood,
but the bull is heading to right where she's stood.
I shall hop over the fence and cut off the corner,
or I won't get there in time and I do need to warn her.

I hold down the wire but get hooked by the crotch,
I used to jump over, but I've lost my touch.
I am balanced quite lightly with feet on tip toes,
with the barbs stuck quite firmly on to my clothes.

I fiddle and pull and try and break free,
and curse and think why does this happen to me?
My wellies are sinking, the material's stuck tight.
I struggle and twist, I'm wrapped up in my plight.

I hear the bull snort and my jeans give a rip,
they have torn from the crotch right round to my hip.
I race off with my stick to save Mrs Smith,
and I shout out to tell her I'll be there in a jiff.

But I needn't have worried, she's the bull by the ring.
She's leading him home on a frayed bit of string.
He's walking behind her just like a wee lamb.
She's in total control, she don't give a damn.

She looks at my trousers splattered with blood,
with my knickers protruding, covered in mud.
She hands me the bull as if he was a kitten,
I pick up the string that was wrapped round her mitten.

Next day on my doorstep I find a small box,
right in the top is a new pair of socks.
And carefully wrapped is a new pair of knickers
still in a packet and covered in stickers.

Handwritten with care she'd left a short letter.
She thought that my leg should soon get much better.
She said that she hoped I'd avoid barbed wire fences,
and would pray that next time I would use all my senses!

Wild Scotland.

Written after a glorious week's holiday in and around Fort William.

Majestic, soaring mountains,
muddied, heathered slopes.
Mist seeping through the hillsides,
the land of dreams and hopes.

Sweeping glens and valleys,
lochs smudged with passing clouds.
Gushing streams and waterfalls,
far from the bustling crowds.

Distant offshore islands,
where eagles scan the skies.
Wild untamed and glorious,
a balm for weary eyes.

Noble stags with antlers,
proud lords of untamed lands.
Thousands of windswept acres,
untouched by human hands.

Gnarled and ancient forests,
the legends that they hide.
The clans and stone walled castles,
protect the land with pride.

The harsh raw edge of winter,
softened by drifting snow.
Squat isolated farmsteads,
with firesides all aglow.

The tartans tell the history,
of those who've gone before.
Strong kilted men with bagpipes,
play tunes from days of yore.

This ancient land is precious,
a pure sanctuary of peace.
We must always be respectful,
it is only ours on lease.

Sherborne.

This is my local town. It is full of beautiful historic buildings with a glorious Abbey at the centre. This poem is a gentle reminder of how lucky we are to live in such an idyllic place.

Sherborne is a lovely town,
start at the top and work on down.
The abbey stands right at the heart,
it has been there from near the start.

And many come from far and wide
to see its treasures from inside.
The cobbled streets, the little lanes.
The one way streets, sometimes a pain.

The little buildings crowded in,
the churches there to save our sin.
The quirky buildings, centuries old,
the stories that sometimes unfold.

The public schools attract the best,
a fact the Gryphon might contest.
The unique shops still hanging on,
some say they may soon all be gone.

The castle built for Walter Raleigh,
the pubs each with a skittle alley.
Pageant gardens neat and tidy,
chip shops full to burst on Friday.

Trains that run near every hour,
castle gardens for every flower.
Sports halls, centres, pools and pitches,
some say it's all for the richest.

Digby estates, lords of the manor.
Proudly flying their own banner.
The Terraces just up the hill,
The Yeatman if you're feeling ill.

Pack Monday Fair to buy your tat.
A furry bear, a knitted hat.
So many they do like to moan
about the town that they call home.

They say it's full of older folk,
and charity shops are just a joke.
They laugh at those who say Sherbun
I know it's just a bit of fun.

But we should really stand up tall,
we're better than some shopping mall.
Be proud to say it's your home town
and don't just always run it down!

The Shire.

I couldn't leave you without a mention of my roots!

Worcestershire is where I began,
the county where the sauce is from.
Meanders of the River Severn,
The Malvern Hills so close to heaven.

The Vale of Evesham drips with plums,
where bees on wing make noisy hums.
Worcester's buildings, black and white.
The cathedral towers to dizzy heights.

Redditch is where I went to school,
we had to do things by the rule.
It's where I learned of verbs and nouns
it's now a bustling growing town.

And Edward Elgar gave us all
music to fill the Albert Hall.
The county that I call my shire,
with country lanes and towering spires.

From north to south the road runs fast.
And some may stop, but most drive past.
But this is where are all my roots,
the county famous for its fruits.

And I have moved and gone away,
but maybe I'll go back some day.
And have a look at our old place,
and see old friends face to face.

At The End Of The Day.

No regrets!

At the end of the day
when the sun's burning low,
and the path you are on
has nowhere left to go.

When you reach out your hand
and bid this world goodbye,
will you know you have lived
and have no need to cry?

Will your mind be full up
with the memories that you made?
Will you know that you tried
when your light starts to fade?

Did you live your life full?
Did you grasp it with both hands?
Did you set off and explore
those far, distant lands?

Will you have no regrets?
Did you learn how to see?
The beauty of nature
in each leaf on a tree.

Did you find one to love
with each breath that you took?
Did you laugh 'till you cried?
Did you read a good book?

Did you give all your heart
and your body and soul,
can you hold your head high
when the drum starts to roll?

Now is your time
it never is too late.
Don't put off your dreams,
they won't always wait.

Seize life whilst you can,
we have but one chance.
If you have to face rain clouds
just learn how to dance!

My Promise.

And finally, for my family.

When you feel there is no hope.
When you feel you cannot cope.
When the darkness closes in,
when your light is burning dim.

When your heart feels it will burst,
when you feel your life is cursed.
When you have nowhere to go,
when you have taken blow on blow.

I will push away the night,
I will guide you with a light.
I will hug your tears away,
I will be here, I will stay.

Do not feel that you're alone,
I will be your stepping stone.
I will hug you when you cry,
I will show you how to fly.

I'll be your hope when all seems lost.
I'll light the stars and melt the frost.
I'll show you that I really care,
I'll give my heart for you to share.

Lightning Source UK Ltd.
Milton Keynes UK
UKHW020806050121
376402UK00008B/105